INTERIOR DESIGNERS
SHOWCASE OF
COLOR

First published in the United States of America by:
Rockport Publishers, Inc.
146 Granite Street
Rockport, Massachusetts 01966
Telephone: (508) 546-9590
Fax: (508) 546-7141
Telex: 5106019284 ROCKORT PUB

Distributed to the book trade and art trade in the U.S. and Canada by:
AIA Press
1735 New York Avenue NW
Washington, DC 20006
(800) 365-2724

Other Distribution by:
Rockport Publishers, Inc.
Rockport, Massachusetts 01966

ISBN 1-55835-112-4

10 9 8 7 6 5 4 3 2 1

Art Director: *Stephen Bridges*
Designer: *Laura Herrmann*
Editor: *Rosalie Grattaroti*
Production Manager: *Barbara States*
Typesetting: *FinalCopy, Newburyport, MA*

Printed in Singapore

▶ ▶ ▸

INTERIOR DESIGNERS'
SHOWCASE OF
COLOR

By Melanie & John Aves

The American Institute of Architects Press
Washington, D.C.

▼

CONTENTS

(LEFT) *The richness of a faux finish painted wall with cascades of sumptuous drapery, accents of off-white in the mantle and inlaid chair and the soft glow of old gold creates an elegant color plan reminiscent of a luxurious past.*
— RONN JAFFE

INTRODUCTION

MELANIE & JOHN AVES

Color is the most powerful decorating element in our homes. Color is memorable. Color is above all personal.

The purpose of *Interior Designers' Showcase of Color* is to demonstrate how world-class interior designers use color to create rooms which reflect the style and preferences of their clients and to inform the reader about color and its effects in interior design. With this inspiration and understanding, you can create your own special style.

Over the years, we have experienced great pleasure in planning colors for our living spaces. As young newlyweds we painted our first apartment white from corner to corner and hung a large oil painting in the middle of the living room. This became the color palette for that room. A blue damask fabric stretched across one wall of our bedroom established the color scheme for that space, and a hand-me-down kitchen table painted red became the color for the kitchen. A white background made all this improvisation possible and allowed us to evolve as our tastes developed. Our budget was less than $1,000, and it was probably the most satisfying home we've ever colored.

With today's technology in paint mixing, our choices of paint color are infinite. The incredible shrinking globe has given us more fabrics from more fibers, more floor coverings and wall coverings and more decorative accessories available at every price level than ever before. Deciding exactly what we would like to come home to, how we will paint and arrange our very own cave is a much more complicated task than ever before. An understanding of color can really help us achieve the goal of a pleasant, personal and comfortable home. In chapter seven, we've given suggestions on how to create mood with color to help you

achieve your own desired "look." And it need not cost a king's ransom to create original and expressive spaces.

Through our association with fine furniture, fabric and accessories marketers for over two decades, we have been able to witness the evolution of fashion trends from the top of the elite trade-only furnishings industry to the retail floor. Our experiences working with color as a painter and as a ceramacist have contributed to our interest and response to color. Our work in the area of education has made us aware of how a little information on color theory can open the doors to the magnificent possibilities available to everyone.

Our point of view is that there aren't any trends or rules that are more important than genuine personal expression. There are hundreds of options but only one decision maker that matters. You. The people who eat and sleep, entertain, play and rejuvenate in the spaces are the ones whose well-being is affected. The examples of professional interior designers' work with color could be imitated but would better be used as a starting point for developing a genuine personal palette of your own.

Enjoy color. Take these tips from the professionals and then be creative. Think about the people who will be in your home who matter the most. Imagine the things you'll do together and alone.

Remember: Color is above all personal.

HOW PROFESSIONALS SELECT A COLOR PALETTE

1-14

Interior designers are experts at combining colors in original ways, and each project requires a new and creative mix reflecting the personality and preferences of the client.

Designers choose color schemes based on the client's wardrobe, skin and hair color as well as favorite antiques and accessories. Plans are also developed around works of art, the views of surrounding landscapes and gardens, as well as backdrops for personal collections. Some designers are known for their signature color palettes which reflect their individual perspectives and preferences. The palettes are modified from project to project, but the stamp of the designer's style is always present and sometimes results in the beginning of design trends. Other designers change palettes at will to fit the needs of the individual project and each client's personality.

(ABOVE) A monochromatic oatmeal colored plan creates serenity in this Kips Bay Showhouse bedroom.
— BILLY FRANCIS

(RIGHT) Wildflower violet, this fresh color is both captivating and serene in a memorable Saladino bedroom.
— JOHN SALADINO

1-7

1-1

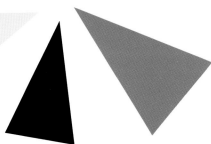

(ABOVE) *Steve Chase is especially recognized for his use of neutrals and natural materials. This room combines textured natural fabrics with stone, wood, marble and oxidized copper for turquoise accents.* — STEVE CHASE

STEVE CHASE

Steve Chase is an internationally recognized designer who has been widely published and has designed personal spaces around the world on the ground (residences), in the air (planes), and afloat (yachts). Known for his sensitive use of natural materials and colors, he especially favors tones from the desert where he makes his home.

"I am very partial to color and to almost all colors. I feel color is coming back, although we use a lot of beige and neutrals in our work. My highest preference is a slightly gray-beige. We use a lot of taupe and make-up tan (a very dirty tan, make-up color)."

1-2

1-3

(ABOVE) *This living space uses colors and materials from the desert environment.* — STEVE CHASE

(LEFT) *Chase is capable of customizing a palette to suit the client's taste and style. Shown here, a beautifully balanced complementary color scheme using red and green.* — STEVE CHASE

(RIGHT) *Chase's bright and playful strong colors prove his virtuosity.* — STEVE CHASE

JOHN SALADINO

Internationally recognized designer John Saladino's work is distinguished by subtle neutral colors which evoke a sophisticated serenity; a feeling of timeless luxury. He creates variety through texture and accents with deep and vibrant tones. Saladino's work is strongly influenced by neoclassic architecture, particularly the work of Andrea Palladio in the 16th Century. "I like visual and classical quotations" – a historical reference. His emphasis on large scale classical form prompts him to keep color intensity low (sorbet colors) with subtle changes from light to dark. The mood he creates is often cool and restful.

1-5

1-6

(ABOVE) *This delicate neutral scheme combines smoke grey with persimmon red to celebrate the architecture of the living area.* — JOHN SALADINO

(RIGHT) *An airy blue and cloud white combine to lift the heavier wood tones of this room in classic Saladino style.* — JOHN SALADINO

Mario Buatta

"My approach is to reflect the client's taste – interiors should be colorful, comfortable and conducive to the way they live their lives."

Mario Buatta is especially attentive to his client's style; the way they dress, their collections, their pastimes. He creates colorful settings which effuse the personality of their owners. The color palette will evolve gradually. "I feel that a house should grow in the same way an artist's painting grows, a few dabs today, a few more tomorrow and the rest when the spirit moves you. When the painting is completed (as no room ever is!), it never reflects the artist's original vision. A room should come together through this process, as the people living in it grow, and where their needs and paths take them."

1-9

1-8

(ABOVE) *One side of an English country bedroom in traditional blue and white with touches of coral and green by the inimitable 'prince of chintz'.* — **Mario Buatta**

(RIGHT) *Warm eggplant as a dramatic neutral for a romantic color palette with much contrast from dark to light.* — **Mario Buatta**

BILLY FRANCIS

Billy Francis is known to have a special eye for selecting the best of different periods and styles. When mixing the old and new, he claims "the exact balance depends on the client . . . but the aim is always quality and above all, comfort."

Although his reputation is that of "Houston's society designer", Billy Francis' domestic interiors can be found in California, Florida, Acapulco and London.

Francis is a color virtuoso; his sensitivity to the nuances of various color relationships is evident in each room that he creates.

1-12

(ABOVE) *Red and white patterned wallpaper, yellow upholstered chair cushions and blue and white porcelain skillfully balanced to create a friendly atmosphere for elegant dining.*
— **BILLY FRANCIS**

(RIGHT) *The garden colors are all brought together on the cheerful table.* — **BILLY FRANCIS**

(LEFT) *Butter cream yellow, rose pink and sisal floor-covering glow in an intimate living space.* — **BILLY FRANCIS**

1-13

1-10

SALLY SIRKIN LEWIS

Sally Sirkin Lewis uses strong contrasts and natural colors to create dynamic contemporary interiors. A Los Angeles based designer with a worldwide practice, Ms. Lewis offers the following clues to her standards:

▲ Space: Affords the mind time to think and explore; to dream fantasies and envision realities.

▲ Symmetry: Invokes the classics and balances the universe.

▲ Understatement: Brings tranquility and refinement to our lives.

▲ Art: Enriches our souls.

▲ Quality: Is everlasting.

Design: the sum of the above."

(ABOVE) *Impact is achieved with opposing black and ivory then moderated with middle tones of vanilla and straw. This vignette by a highly skilled Los Angeles designer demonstrates the power of contrasting neutrals.*
— SALLY SIRKIN LEWIS

(LEFT) *Sally Sirkin Lewis's black leather upholstery and neutral backgrounds are an ideal setting for the art and artifacts in the designer's own home.*
— SALLY SIRKIN LEWIS

1-11

SPECIAL EFFECTS

Professional designers create palettes with personality by considering all of the large surface areas in a space. It is easy to overlook the color impact of ceilings and floors. The source of light, whether natural or artificial, impacts all other color decisions.

New York designer Marvin Affrime explains, "We consider color a 'tool' to work with in developing our interiors, just as wood, paper, fabric and marble are tools of our profession. We start each project by developing colored plans and elevations which exploit the shape, form, rhythm, mood and character of the environment. Then, we interpret the colors through materials and finishes. (Example: a floor shown in beige might become blonde wood, travertine marble, limestone, carpet or simply paint). Ditto for each other color in each other location drawn on our colored plans and elevations."

1-17

CEILINGS

Dramatic effects can be created on ceilings quite economically with a sensitive choice of paint color. There are also many more elaborate ceiling treatments which will contribute to the artistic coherence of color in a room. Here is a collection of imaginative suggestions from the pros:

▲ Metallic colors to carry out architectural detailing and to create a shimmering, sparkling effect.

▲ A color similar to the walls but lighter to make a small room seem bigger.

▲ A full chroma secondary color in a recessed lighted cove for dramatic accent.

▲ Light lacquer to reflect and disperse prismatic uplighting.

▲ A grid of wood to put on the ceiling and paint a background color behind it, perhaps a green, perhaps an aqua blue.

▲ Glazing and faux finishes to achieve depth and interest.

▲ Painting ceilings like the sky with clouds and stars.

▲ Using dark colors to make ceilings "disappear."

▲ Painting with pale washed out blue or pale apricot to create Georgia O'Keeffe sky colors.

1-24

(RIGHT) *In the Atlanta Symphony Decorators' Show House, "an ugly attic opening that existed prior to the improvements was turned into a positive by tenting up into the attic space through the opening to create a trey ceiling effect. Using a shirred fabric in blue reinforcing a feeling of outdoor sky, the space increased in volume . . . reinforcing the depth of space through the application of cool colors."* — REBECCA STAHR

(OPPOSITE) *Custom painted mural creates a trompe l'oeil ceiling with blue sky and clouds to oversee the walls depicting a beautiful garden complete with lily pond in this fantasy bedroom.* — RONN JAFFE

(LEFT) *The palest hint of green in this circular ceiling balances the peach in the carpet and upholstery and contributes to the light and airy feeling of a room brightened by windows overlooking garden foliage.*
— GAY MATTHAEI

▲ For drama - gold or silver leafing.

▲ Using a color different from the walls to adjust the height higher or lower.

▲ Painting patterns on the ceiling to add vitality.

▲ Painting ceilings pale blue with white moldings to look like the sky.

▲ Using natural wood tones in a light palette range to prevent the feeling that the ceiling is closing in on you.

▲ Art on the ceiling to distract and relax.

▲ Stippling color in the center to create depth.

▲ Same color as walls with molding between painted in accent colors.

▲ Using ceiling color which reflects or complements the floor color creates a strong interplay.

▲ Gold or silver tea papers.

▲ Painting the ceiling of an outdoor type of room the color of nature, a softly mottled blue-green on a white ground.

▲ White is still the best choice, but carrying wall color or wall covering to the ceiling adds warmth.

▲ Extending ceiling color down the walls to a horizontal line; for example, stopping at the chair rail to play up the wainscot below.

1-21

(ABOVE) *A strong buttercup yellow lifts the spirits in beautiful combination with deep green walls in a hospitable dining room.* — **DEBRA BLAIR**

(RIGHT) *Floor and ceiling in rich green frame this cozy space.* — **CHERYL DRIVER**

1-27

1-25

1-19

(FAR LEFT) An unusual "star-lit" mirrored ceiling energizes this living room. — CAROL MELTZER

(LEFT) Victorian antiques are happy with romantic fabrics repeated on furniture and rafters.
— ALLISON HOLLAND

(BELOW LEFT) The ceiling painted in peach spreads a romantic glow over the ruffles and flourishes of this elegant bedroom. — ALLISON HOLLAND

(BELOW) A red ceiling provides contrast with the aged coloring of pine paneling in this rich combination of memorable color. — MARJORIE SLOVACK

(OPPOSITE) Pale azure blue combines harmoniously with a natural wood ceiling finished in honey-tones.
— ALLISON HOLLAND

1-22

1-28

(RIGHT) *Convex glass block window makes rainbows on white tile surfaces at different times of day according to season.* — **LOIS BLACK**

(BELOW) *The lace and linen covered willow bed floats in the center of an attic bedroom with painted walls and ceiling of pale periwinkle blue and periwinkle and white stripe wall covering. The floor is hand painted canvas in bottle green with ferns and botanicals of violets and other woodland flowers.* — **VIVIAN IRVINE**

1-26

1-23

FLOORS

A second large area that must be carefully integrated into the color plan for a room is the floor. A floor, unlike the untouched ceiling, has limitations because it *will* be touched, used and soiled by people and animals. A floor must be practical as well as aesthetically pleasing. It must be durable and cleanable. Because floor surface treatments are expensive and often stay with the home when owners move, they should be adaptable to work with a variety of color plans. Professionals make the following comments regarding floor color:

▲ I prefer neutral floor colors — why draw attention to the floor, when wonderful furniture or art is being used above that plane. I truly believe that backgrounds should be backgrounds — to act as an environment for the wonderful things within the space.

▲ Here in the West we use a lot of granite which is very costly. We use travertine which is not so costly. We use a lot of tile which tends to be quite inexpensive.

▲ Large size tiles (18-24") can be very effective.

▲ I love a honey-colored and old-looking wood floor.

▲ Carpeting is delustered and more textural in lighter and more neutral colors.

▲ Wood: I prefer medium to dark floors. They just seem more classic.

▲ Tile: Neutrals, naturals and terra-cotta; whites in bathrooms.

▲ Carpet: Neutrals again - sisal types especially easy to work with.

▲ We advise clients that items which have a long life span or are costly to replace are best suited for neutral colors.

▲ Area rugs over wood or stone/marble floors.

▲ Earth tones and greens especially; we tend to like darker colors on floors to 'anchor' them and lighter ceilings which reflect better. Just look outside and you'll see why! It is difficult to improve on nature.

▲ Wood: Bleached and rubbed. No dark floors.

▲ Medium to dark colors. The light colors can look very pretty but are impractical to keep clean.

▲ Early 19th Century hand embroidered carpets, faded Turkish kilims, a good sheared low pile industrial carpet fitted wall to wall. Leather bound sisal or sea grass area rugs and hall runners all offer the opportunity to go traditional or eclectic.

▲ I rarely use tile except in tropical climates.

(BELOW) *Custom contemporary carpet with tones of blue pattern on subtle neutrals defines the dining space and establishes the color theme.* — JAMES ESSARY

1-30

1-29

(RIGHT) Papered ceiling suggests foliage overhead and patterned carpet repeats the woodsy theme.
— MARJORIE SLOVACK

(RIGHT) Memorable black marble floor with central pattern establishes color theme for bathroom.
— LILA LEVINSON

(OPPOSITE) The high ceilings and dramatic windows of this space are lifted by the white monochromatic plan, anchored on a candy-stripe surprise. An all-white space usually appears contemporary even if some of the furnishings are traditional.
— VINCENT MOTZEL AND ARIEL SANS

1-32

MORE ABOUT FLOORS...

▲ Darker wood floors seem to be right with most furnishings. Carpeting in the way of area rugs adds softness and warmth to a room.

▲ Carpets that are highly patterned and strong in color are my preference.

▲ What is actually happening is a return to an appreciation of the rich natural fibers and elements. This is evidenced by the growing market for granite, marble, inlaid hardwood and wool carpet for floors.

▲ Dark floors (wood, stone, painted, etc.) complement rugs best especially antique or patterned ones. In wood, the finish may be from tetre-negre to warm brown. In stone, I prefer deep earth tones again to set off brighter colored rugs. Of course, a white stone or marble floor is wonderful in a tropical climate.

▲ From my view of the world in Southern California, the best floor colors are evolving from the bleached light look to natural neutrals and dramatic charcoals.

▲ I use very little ceramic tile, but I love the look of natural stones ranging from flagstone in Mexican Conchuella stone to limestone and European marbles. These natural stones inspire a color palette in the neutral range: from taupe to clay to charcoal and black; although contrasting neutrals can be very dramatic.

▲ Although I've always favored neutrals, I'm starting to introduce more color through patterns, borders and banding of contrasting (albeit subdued) color.

▲ For a beach house, I used yellow, cream and sky blue carpet on travertine floors - it worked with all the rooms, and the pattern resembled waves.

▲ For a contemporary look, the more neutral the better. However, with traditional looks, deep wood tones are best especially with a strong patterned area rug.

▲ Italian mosaic tiles are great for kitchen and bath.

▲ I feel there is a tremendous trend toward full blown floral European style patterned wall-to-wall carpeting, currently.

▲ Any middle value since they tend to best hide foot prints. Textures or grain are what I rely on for easy maintenance. I primarily install waxed wood floors, natural stone or natural wool carpets

HALLWAYS

Professional designers use color to bring vitality to spaces which are really "pass throughs." Imaginative color planning in a hallway can convey friendliness, excitement or mystery inviting further exploration. The entry or reception hall may introduce the color theme of a home and create harmony between various spaces.

(BELOW) *The optimism of yellow and vivid flowers combine on this handpainted wallcovering energizing a narrow hallway and adjacent room. The drawing and the color are Chinese derivatives and denote special status.*
— ALLISON HOLLAND

(OPPOSITE) *A ruby red entry hall trimmed in white looks dressed up for company.*
— GILLIAN DRUMMOND

1-38

1-37

(OPPOSITE) *Sky blue carpet and white architectural detail create a heavenly reception hall.*
— JIM WESTERFIELD

(LEFT) *A collector of contemporary sculpture needs neutral backgrounds. Depth and interest are added by the painted faux finish on the walls and the severe polished black floor.* — MEL LOWRANCE

(BELOW) *The strong blue of the walls is a perfect complement to the beautiful dark finished wood of the gleaming bare floors in this hallway. Elegant art and accessories line the passage and carry the eye back into the space. With no natural light source, the room conveys great vitality.*
— JANET SCHIRN

THE PRIMARIES

The primary colors are the three basic hues red, blue and yellow. They are the foundation of the color wheel, and theoretically, all other colors are mixed from them. The primaries are universal and timeless. They appear in some form in every historical period as well as in most styles of interior design. It is important to be familiar with the positions of the primaries on the color wheel and the relationships formed by these positions.

Color Wheel

In the color wheel at the right, the primaries form a triangle with equal sides within the circle, and the secondaries form another triangle. Each color has a "complement" which is located directly across from it on the wheel. Thus, green is the complement of red; orange is the complement of blue; violet is the complement of yellow and so on.

A perfectly balanced color scheme might use equal parts of three colors which are equidistant on the color wheel. But the colors as they appear on the wheel are pure, and in larger areas might be too intense to create a comfortable environment for living. Interior designers often compensate for intensity by tinting (adding white) to at least one of the colors in a color scheme or by graying (adding the complementary color). In these ways they may create contrast through a change in value (lightness and darkness) or intensity (brightness and dullness). With even this limited information, it is easy to see how the possibilities for combining colors are infinite and inviting. See *Chapter 9 – Altering Color* for more ideas.

If you study the photograph shown at the top of the following page, you will see that the designer has used the primaries for the basic color scheme. The naturally lightest hue, yellow, is chosen for the large areas of the walls and tinted even lighter to create a quietly cheerful sunlit effect. The ceiling is painted white to help reflect light and balance the darker wood tones in the trim and furniture. Blue is the dominant color in the furnishings. Its brilliance is softened and enriched by appearing with white in the fabric on the sofa and draperies and with yellow on the rug. A glowing red is used for accent on the tufted piece in the foreground and the two armchairs by the bay window. The total effect is lively and pleasing but not overwhelming, a beautifully colored room.

2-1

(LEFT) *Red, blue and yellow are balanced in intensity and arrangement to establish freshness in a classic setting.*
— **CHARLOTTE MOSS**

2-3

2-4

(RIGHT) *Upholstery in primary tones lifts the spirit of this traditional home.*
— **ALLISON HOLLAND**

(FAR RIGHT) *Sunshine yellow and vivid blue interplay to create a promising place to start the day. The coordination of each detail and the layering of pattern on pattern have the effect of great depth, and a sense of comfort.*
— **MARILYNN LUNDY**

(LEFT) *The spectrum moves from the wall to the chairs launching dynamic dining possibilities.*
— TONY SUTTON

(ABOVE) *Jewel tones on silk cushions, vivid upholstery and contemporary art contrast elegantly in an eclectic black and white area.* — SUZANNE TUCKER AND TIMOTHY MARKS

(LEFT) *Soft tones of the three primaries combine gracefully in this traditional setting.* — KENNETH HOCKIN

2-18

(FAR LEFT) *Red, yellow and blue create a spirit of fun in this engaging room.*
— AL EVANS

(LEFT) *Whimsical primary and secondary colors create exciting and friendly surroundings for children.*
— LISE LAWSON

(BELOW) *The joy of pure, bright, primary and secondary colors makes them a perfect choice for children's spaces.*
— DANIELLE GARR

(OPPOSITE) *A vivid painting and panoramic water view suggest a primary palette with watermelon red upholstery played against an airy green and white carpet.*
— CORNELIA COVINGTON SMITHWICK

2-2

2-6

2-7

(ALL) *Different values of vibrant electric blue and accents of pure red and yellow bring liveliness to a minimalist contemporary apartment.*
— ROBERT KLEINSCHMIDT

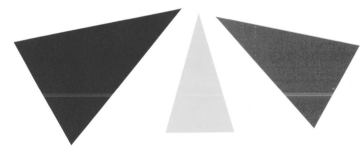

2-20

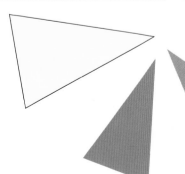

(BOTH) *A skillful balance of primary colors seems reserved when the pure
hues are tinted and the intensity is slightly lowered.* — **DEBRA BLAIR**

2-10

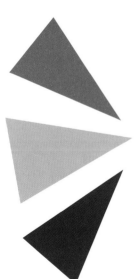

(LEFT) *Chalk-like tinted primaries provide subtle richness and balance with darker wood tones.* — **M.B. Affrime**

(BELOW LEFT) *A softly orchestrated symphony of primary tones makes this living room a place to linger.* — **Kenneth Hockin**

(BELOW) *A primary yellow background unifies an intense and complex color scheme with accents of red and blue.* — **Jean Valente**

2-9

2-17

(RIGHT) *Pale white washed paneled walls provide a muted background for the rich blues, and vibrant pinks and yellows of this living room.*
— SUZANNE TUCKER AND TIMOTHY MARKS

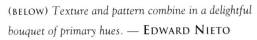

2-19

2-11

(ABOVE) *All three primaries in lower intensity knit together a place of quiet comfort.* — DEBRA BLAIR

(RIGHT) *A masterfully light touch of pure red, sky blue, a hint of yellow and apple green against airy white walls creates an exquisite balance in this traditional bedroom showing off the rich wood finishes.* — JAMES ESSARY

2-16

PRIMARILY RED

Red is the most dramatic, emotional and active of the three primaries. It is an especially versatile color in its effects, enlivening interior spaces by creating excitement, warmth and elegance. The use of red suggests a bold and confident attitude. Living with red can be satisfying in almost any space, but it is less often used in sleeping areas because of its energizing quality. When tinted, it becomes distinctively feminine; when deepened, it is more rich and masculine; when used with yellow, the cheerful orange family is created, and when combined with blue, the more dreamy and mysterious violets are created. The complement of red is green.

Diverse cultures view red in very different ways. The Chinese have always favored red, traditionally using it for the bridal gown, a sign of longevity. The Romans used it to symbolize power, an association that has been continued in the rituals of the Catholic church. Many nations have chosen red for their flags. In recent political history, it has often been a symbol of more radical political activism. Emotionally, red is understood as a symbol of anger as well as embarrassment. In our culture, the attention-getting qualities of red are often used as an alert for danger.

In nature, red is associated with blood, the powerful life-sustaining fluid and with the earth where certain types of soil and rocks are characterized by this distinctive color. Fruits, flowers, foliage and many vegetables tempt us with appealing red. Eve succumbed to the charm of the color of the forbidden fruit even before sampling the taste.

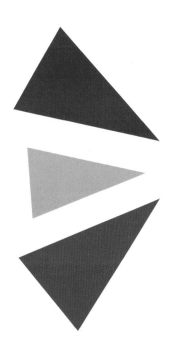

2-31c

(RIGHT) An unusual tone of red paint almost the color of a bright clay is ideal for a comfortable and stylish living area. Rich blue stripes combine with red on the upholstery fabric and a pale golden carpet completes the balanced color triangle. — E. MORRISON BROWN

2-26

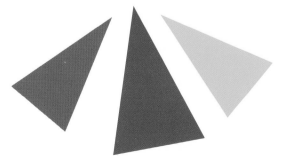

(LEFT) *Red fantasy finish on walls is offset by silk pillows in natural greens, yellows and earth tones. A high style study in contrasts.* — RITA ST. CLAIR

(BELOW) *Just the right brick red is a perfect feature color for these traditional living spaces.* — KATHLEEN BUOYMASTER

2-30

(ALL) *A carefully chosen red is used extensively with creamy white in adjacent rooms making stylish and livable spaces.*
— **Allison Holland**

2-22

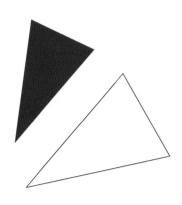

2-23

2-24

(ABOVE) *Reds are particularly appropriate for a bold 18th Century interior, here repeated on the striped wallcovering and patterned fabric.* — BARBARA AND MICHAEL ORENSTEIN

2-31a

(BELOW AND RIGHT) *Hibiscus red covers the cabinets and runs around the moldings that tie the preparation and dining areas of this country kitchen together.*
— ALLISON HOLLAND

(BELOW RIGHT) *Surprising red energizes this bathroom.* — DIANE JUST

2-29

2-28

2-27

PRIMARILY BLUE

Of all the colors, blue is perhaps most universally equated with beauty. It has remained popular from ancient times until the present throughout the world. Blue is timeless, linking the present with tradition and lasting values. One of the three primary hues, it is perhaps the most versatile in its expressive qualities. Its analogous families include greens when mixed with yellow, and violets when mixed with red. The complement of blue is orange.

Blue is most commonly associated with the sky and the sea. Sky blue is sometimes called cerulean or azure, describing a vivid light blue. The blue of the sea is affected by the sky. Depending on depth, time of day, weather conditions and type of ocean floor, the color may range from deep blue-violet to palest aqua.

Blue has the capacity to express the airiness of clouds and the solidity of slate, the calmness of a clear sky as well as electric energy. It can evoke clarity or mystery, joyfulness or sadness, broad daylight or deep night. These effects depend on the amount of white and black in the color, a quality called value; and on the amount of the complement in the color, a quality called intensity.

Psychologically, blue is associated with tranquility and contentment. Deep blue is considered to be the optimum color for meditation, for slowing down the bodily processes to allow relaxation and recuperation. Blue often symbolizes femininity (the Virgin Mary is usually cloaked in blue), quality (blue ribbons) and loyalty (true blue).

In interior design, softer and lighter blues are generally preferred for larger areas. Blue is especially effective as a ceiling color. Stronger and darker tones work well for accents and richness in smaller areas. Because of its calming effects, blue has long been a favorite for bedrooms. Its association with water, cleanliness and order make it popular in kitchens and bathrooms, particularly in combination with white. By itself, blue can seem a bit too cool, aloof and unstimulating. Knowledgeable designers counteract these effects by balancing blue with warmer colors such as red for a strong energizing effect, yellow for freshness and gaiety and peach for luxury and elegance.

2-37

2-46

(ABOVE) *A low intensity medium blue works beautifully with white floor and trim, complementing the honey tones of the large cabinet and picture frames.* — PAT STOTLER

(RIGHT) *The stairwell becomes a feature with naturalistic blue patterned panels dramatically surrounded with one thousand fathom blue-black and accented with warm wood tones.* — ANTHONY ANTINE

(OPPOSITE) *A light-absorbing blue-black wall focuses attention on the brighter art and is balanced by more intense tones of blue in the furniture coverings.*
— ANTHONY ANTINE

2-36

(RIGHT) *A ceiling painted blue heightens the serene, cool blues of the tile counter, fabric and other trim. The pale wood tones of the cabinets are of a similar intensity.* — **MARCIA MORINE**

(BELOW RIGHT) *The gentle blue repeated in damask, plaid, print and carpet seems to reflect in a pickled wood finish, offering a serene place to enjoy reading.* — **ELAINE BASS**

(BELOW) *The vivid blue is used carefully, the white carpet and ceiling balance the stronger darker tones, and the result is stunning.* — **KENNETH HOCKIN**

2-41

2-43

2-35

(RIGHT) *Welcome to breakfast in blue dominated floral prints and garden-themed accessories. A soft blue can act as a neutral behind an array of brighter colors.*
— LISA WEITZ

(BELOW) *Exquisite blue walls in combination with white suggest a French influence, and lend authenticity to a gourmet kitchen. The unusual deep blue appliance color adds style and richness.* — LILA LEVINSON

(BELOW RIGHT) *The deep blue of a night sky is balanced with crisp white trim to establish a cheerful, comforting mood for a bedroom.* — STEPHANIE WALTERS

2-38

2-46b

2-34

2-33

(ABOVE) *Dress formal blue silk with purple evokes a high-key mood in a contemporary living area.*
— DIANE JUST

(LEFT) *A deep blue and white wall-papered ceiling is reflected back in a richly toned rug, counter tops and artwork lends drama and elegance to an efficient culinary center.*
— GAIL WILKINS

(ABOVE) *Change in lightness and darkness creates a dramatic and exciting contemporary living room. The deep Prussian blue walls are balanced with a white ceiling and trim, light toned furnishings and the dash of a custom contemporary carpet.* — JAMES ESSARY

(RIGHT) *Periwinkle blue with crisp borders of white flows to a black and white kitchen in which the blue from the family room is repeated on a plate collection.*
— JILL VAN TOSH

2-39b

2-32

2-40

2-42

(ABOVE) *A soft periwinkle blue dominates the upholstery fabric against a warm white background. Art, accessories and flowers elaborate the theme.* — JUDY HOWARD

(ABOVE LEFT) *Classic powder blue with dressy white trim showcases a variety of airy blue and pink patterns and textures in upholstery and collected needlework.* — RONALD BRICKE

(LEFT) *Completely feminine blue and white plaid accompanies pink and blue floral garlands with green leaves on soft white ground. A practical deep blue carpet and pink accents make this a room for a little girl to dream dreams in.* — JAMES ESSARY

PRIMARILY YELLOW

Yellow is a powerful color, both light in value and extremely intense in its purest form. Its brilliance is most often associated with the sun and evokes a sense of energy and excitement. In interior spaces, these qualities may need to be subdued through tinting, dulling or by combining with other colors. The emotional effects of yellow are optimistic and bright, yet sometimes unsettling and seldom restful. Yellow combines with red to form the warm family of oranges and with blue to blend the cooler greens. Its complement is violet.

Gold as a part of the yellow family is responsible for the association of richness and opulence with this brilliant color. Metallic gold was especially popular during the Renaissance in the decorative arts, serving as an accent and a background for other rich strong colors. The ochres, notoriously unstable and subject to fading, have been an integral part of artistic palettes since Prehistoric times.

In Eastern cultures, yellow has always been a revered color. The Brahmans considered it sacred, and in India, brides wore yellow as they had in ancient Rome. The Chinese associated this color with royalty and deity. However, in the West, yellow has quite different connotations. At various times in Western history it has been symbolically associated with heretics, with deceit as personified by portrayals of Judas Escariot, with illness through yellow crosses identifying the plague, with cowardice (yellow streak), and with caution (yellow lights).

Yellow is a perennial favorite in interior design, combining with greens to suggest natural freshness, with blue for the effect of cleanliness and brightness and with red for gaiety and richness. When tinted, its brightness may be subdued, but it retains an appealing liveliness. When its intensity is lowered through the addition of violet tones, it becomes earthy and reassuring. Like the other primaries, yellow can evoke a variety of responses. Its versatility has ensured its place in color schemes of virtually every recorded decorative period.

(BELOW) *Glazed butter yellow walls and ceiling cheerfully illuminate a small room with minimal natural light.* — JACK CLARK

2-47

(BOTH) *A delicate tint of butterscotch looks exactly right as a background for antique furnishings and a rich yellow floral bedcover. The white pillows and woodwork add sparkle to a monochromatic color scheme.* — **ALLISON HOLLAND**

2-49

2-48

2-60

2-50

(ABOVE) *Yellow and green are skillfully combined to create this pleasantly bright bathroom.* — BARBARA AND MICHAEL ORENSTEIN

(RIGHT) *Cheerful night or day, this bedroom and sitting room is light and classical. Green is a natural friend of yellow, relating to sunshine and healthy plants.*
— MELINDA DOUGLAS

(ABOVE) *Taffy yellow is an imaginative color choice for a kitchen, flowing smoothly along curving cabinet walls and ceiling in a delicious richness which is functional as well as sophisticated.* — GAIL SHIELDS-MILLER

(RIGHT) *Palest yellow-orange combines with mist green accessories to create an unusual and enchanting retreat by the fire.* — LISA ROSE

2-58

2-59

2-55

2-54

(LEFT) *Palest taffy yellow unifies this living room and is accented by a vivid blue painting inside and a view of the pool and landscape outside.*
— PAT STOTLER

(RIGHT) *A perfect medium blue chair brings life to a soft yellow bedroom. The blue is gently repeated with yellow in the window treatment.* — KENNETH HOCKIN

(FAR RIGHT) *Pale aristocratic yellow frames the bright rooms of this well-appointed home. Yellow can be formal or informal, traditional or contemporary, depending on the hue and intensity.* — DEBRA BLAIR

(RIGHT) *The celebration of nature is natural with yellow and green, a botanical theme.*
— ELLEN LEMER KORNEY

(BELOW RIGHT) *Butter yellow with white floor covering and woodwork provides an optimistic background for watermelon red accents in upholstery solids and prints.*
— JAMES ESSARY

(BELOW) *Yellow gives a cheerful welcome. The two tones of yellow in the striped wall-covering are repeated on the wood panel trim.* — LISA WEITZ

2-56

(ABOVE) *Buttery walls, flowery drapes and elegant windows bring the garden to the table. A multi-colored treatment with yellow acting as the neutral.* — NANCY PICKARD

THE SECONDARIES

The secondary group of pure colors are green, orange and violet. They are mixed by combining equal parts of two primaries; red and yellow make orange, blue and yellow form green and red and blue result in violet. Less frequently used than primaries, they have nevertheless appeared in the decorative arts since ancient times.

"Every room needs these 'flavors' for punch," suggests designer Gail Miller.

"Quite often I use softened secondary colors, green, orange and violet . . . some people thrive on them. Bright tones of these colors make great accents in sun washed interiors," advises designer Marilyn F. Lundy of New York City.

(RIGHT) Successful use of color always depends upon careful attention to every detail, from accessories with particularly enriching finishes to the picture frames and fabric trim. Dressing up a room with flowers chosen for their color adds an especially inviting focal point where the entire palette comes together. — MICHAEL ANTHONY

Green

Of the three, green is the superstar in interior design, often used as a dominant room color and in combination with the primaries. Green is unique in its duality; pushed toward yellow it acts as a warm color, and when more blue is present, it becomes a cool tone. In some form, green goes with every other color, making it a natural neutral. Consider the attractiveness of green plants to accessorize interior spaces and share the air. Our eyes appreciate the beauty of this versatile color, associating it with healthy vegetation, soothing shade, quietness and youth. Bright yellow greens recall the miracle of spring. Deep greens suggest elegance and security. There is a strong trend toward the use of green in the early 90s and several fine examples of its use are presented on the following pages.

3-12

3-15

(TOP) A rich dark green harmonizes beautifully with the red tones of the wood finish in this unusual kitchen color scheme. The white floor and ceiling balance the darker hues.
— BRIAN KILLIAN

3-1

(ABOVE) A collector's home in a carefully mixed shade of dark green is enlivened by pale natural wood, bright blue porcelain and white trim. — JANE J. MARSDEN

(RIGHT) Deep green and white complement the warm tones of the woods in the furniture. — LISA ROSE

3-6

3-8

(ABOVE LEFT) *Combinations of spring leaf and pine nee-dle greens ensure that this living room will feel alive night and day and in every season.* — **DEBRA BLAIR**

(ABOVE RIGHT) *An intimate garden-like space is based upon an exceptional floral wallcovering and further developed with painted cabinet finish, fabric and the lighting fixture.* — **LISA WEITZ**

(ABOVE) *Well-developed manners and interests are reflected in this Southern living space, with artfully modulated hues of green on every seat and surface. Although a monochromatic plan, the variety of tones and the mixed patterns prevent monotony.* — DAN CARITHERS

(LEFT) *Outdoor color moves in to suit the Florida climate and lifestyle.* — VINCENT MOTZEL AND ARIEL SANS

3-13

3-5

(LEFT) *Forest green paired with gold sets a stage for the display of rare art, fine furnishings and elegant fabrics. Dark hues of green can easily be arranged to imply wealth and luxury.* — **JEAN VALENTE**

(BELOW) *A very personal space in restful green with botanical references invites long recuperative interludes with favorite friends or a good book.*
— **MELINDA DOUGLAS**

(OPPOSITE) *Careful planning resulted in this intricate play of various green hues and white, with a "guest color" of melon red. Wall color, architectural detail, lamp base and lamp shade, painted furniture, fabric and fabric trim are all threads of this skillfully woven color plan.* — **CHERYL DRIVER**

3-2

3-9

GREEN ◂ ◂ ◂ 67

(ABOVE LEFT) *The very palest green lifts what might otherwise be a heavy atmosphere, evoking the memory of springtime foliage.* — MICHAEL ANTHONY

(ABOVE) *Time worn finishes and faded fabric colors tell a story of deep rooted tradition and highly developed discernment.* — LINDA CHASE

(LEFT) *Captivating grayed green surrounds a dressing table fit for the most elegant lady.* — BECKI COOK

Violet

Violet seems to be a color of emotional contrasts. Its paler tints are unabashedly romantic, delicate, fragile and exquisitely feminine. A "shrinking violet" is a shy and self-effacing personality. Deeper purple denotes strength and power, the color of royalty and of tragedy, of honor and of mourning. Vivid purple is an exciting accent, aubergine is the sophisticated neutral of a comforting retreat. Violet enjoyed widespread popularity in the Gay Nineties of the late Victorian era when aniline dyes made this expressive color more readily available. In the 1980s, it was often included in grayed low contrast color schemes in combination with rose and teal. As pure colors emerge again, beautiful violet is certain to be a player.

3-21

3-19

(ABOVE) *Rich plum red-violet on upholstery and ceiling looks perfect with light finished golden wood in a comfortable arrangement by the fire.* — CHERYL DRIVER

(RIGHT) *Electric purple establishes a romantic and memorable dining area. Contemporary art and accessories complement the strong color theme.* — SCOTT SNYDER

3-16

3-17

3-18

(ABOVE) *A very distinctive San Francisco area bedroom owes its unique warmth to the hues of violet and related blues carried from walls to pillows and into the coordinated bedspread and window treatment.*
— RONALD SCHWARZ

(ABOVE RIGHT) *A high fashion statement in New York begins with the drama of deep violet and contrasting white trim. The color plan is further developed in the floral print upholstery fabric of matching background.*
— DEBRA BLAIR

(RIGHT) *Violet and white plaid forms the backdrop for violet print upholstery and red accents. A delightful, spirit-brightening room.* — ALLISON HOLLAND

(OPPOSITE) *Light violet in pattern and check adds life with deep red accents in a bright traditional room.*
— CHERYL DRIVER

ORANGE

Orange is amazingly versatile; capable of emitting great energy in its purest form and, as an earth tone, it evokes warmth, comfort and reassurance. As a pale tint, it becomes the most flattering color of all to human skin tones. In spite of its oversaturation in the 1960s, orange has maintained a following and promises to be a popular "new" color in the 1990s.

(RIGHT) *A simple and distinctive color solution is a rich peach paint color. Everything else is clean white, adding appropriate mood and dimension to this small space.*
— DEBRA BLAIR

3-25

(RIGHT) Orange creates a most elegant and flattering background for the indulgence of the bath. White columns, ceilings and pristine tub combine with the green of natural foliage to define an inviting and memorable place. — RON FREY

(BELOW) Cinnamon orange, deep and mysterious, contrasts with fresh white to lift the spirit in youthful exuberance with a traditional cachet in Grand Rapids, Michigan. — RON FREY

(BELOW RIGHT) The California climate comes indoors with this temperate mix of peach, orange and green, a grove for resting and reading. — JUDY SIMES AND RICHARD KENARNEY

3-26

3-23

(RIGHT) *Tangerine, you're the one I love! Wood finishes, walls and fabrics flow in a singular color scheme to form a warm and secure living space.* — AL EVANS

(BELOW) *High drama with orange everywhere in varying tones. The excitement and mystery of faraway places is suggested by this dramatic color scheme.* — LILI KRAY

(BELOW RIGHT) *Unusual faux finish walls have a depth and richness in a tone which resembles terra cotta and acts as a neutral backdrop for high tech furniture and accessories with vivid color accents.* — EDWARD NIETO

3-28

3-27

3-30

(ABOVE) *A stained wood finish in varied tones of orange makes a memorable background for neutral furniture and relates to the tile floor and patterned rug.* — EDWARD NIETO

(RIGHT) *The fantasy finish of the walls in deep orange earth tones, brighter chintz fabric and still brighter gold and brass accents in the chair and lighting fixture add up to high drama in this extraordinary Minnesota bathroom. Who said the Midwest is dull?* — WILLIAM BESON

PASTELS

People seem to know immediately whether or not they like pastels. Often these tints are associated with little girls' rooms or bathrooms, although they really are adaptable and can be used to create very sophisticated effects. In the fifties, pastels were believed to be the most livable colors for interiors. They did not intrude and created light, "restful" spaces.

Pastels are simply lighter tints of any hue, white added to red yields pink and light pink is a pastel. There isn't a hard-edged definition for when a color becomes a pastel. One person's pastel blue might be another's sky blue. But for certain, when colors become so light that they almost seem to be white, or seem to suggest a mere breath of color, they are pastel.

Pastel pink might denote youthful femininity, but pastel green in a contemporary setting is very sophisticated. There are stunning examples of pastel palettes both in New York high rise apartments and Midwest nurseries. On the following pages are a few interesting examples of such palettes that may inspire other ideas for creating a unique personal environment.

4-5

(LEFT) *Peach and cream vanilla melt to the consistency of a rich sauce in this Lincoln Plaza, New York, apartment. This is an appropriate background for featuring art and the unembellished figure of rare woods.*
— MARILYNN LUNDY

(OPPOSITE) *Blue in pastel tints is so delicate that it blends with the neutral wood tones and white that dominates this California contemporary home.*
— RUTH LIVINGSTON

(RIGHT) *This vignette, a closeup of an elegant bedroom, focuses on the complimentary deep pink stain on the walls combining with a soft tint of apple green as well as gold, blue and a touch of red for a lively yet traditional palette.*
— **DAVID HOLCOMB**

4-16a

4-1

4-9

(ABOVE) *A palette of sunlight yellow and soft tints of leaf green and cabbage rose pink lend variety and depth to this sitting room/bedroom.* — T. KELLER DONOVAN:

(RIGHT) *A tint of yellow resembling French vanilla ice cream wraps this charming bedroom.*
— ANNE WEINBERG

(ALL) *A series of contemporary apartment rooms. A contemporary New York City apartment is unified with a monochromatic pastel blue-green that is more interesting and cohesive than an all-over neutral, but still very minimalist and architectural in its simplicity.* — **GAIL GREEN AND DAVID ESTREICH**

4-13

4-2

(OPPOSITE) *Pink, so pastel light that it is almost white, enlivens the garden palette of this elegant living room in the Southeast.*

— CORNELIA COVINGTON SMITHWICK

(RIGHT) *The lightest possible tint of pink, matched on the custom painted drop-lid desk, is carefully planned as background for the deeper leaf green and rose reds of this cheerful bedroom and sitting area.*

— MELINDA DOUGLAS

(BELOW): *Medium to light peach stripes are both cheerful and restful as a background for this robust leaf green and floral fabric.* — DEBRA BLAIR

(BELOW RIGHT) *A tint of grey leaning toward lilac combines with cream and soft pink to create this serene retreat.* — ANNE WEINBERG

4-7

4-10

4-16

(ABOVE) *A pastel vignette in which the richness of textural detail is balanced with exquisite delicate color that suggests a civilized style of life.* — BECKI COOK

(LEFT) *The quintessential space for dreaming; clouds of sheer white fabric, soft blue-green walls, sky blue dust ruffle and a rose red accent on the distinctive bench make magic look effortless.* — GAY MATTHAEI

4-15

4-6

(ABOVE) *An interesting antique box collection and a collection of contemporary porcelain ceramics are point and counterpoint to the dominant pastel fabric which quietly circles the color wheel.* — **ELAINE BASS**

(LEFT) *The hot Southwest sun fades nearly all color, which might be the cue for this regional style palette. The full primary range of red, yellow and blue is very quietly repeated in the fabric and the artwork.*
— **STEPHEN TOMAR AND STUART LAMPERT**

4-8

ANALOGOUS AND COMPLEMENTARY COLOR SCHEMES

ANALOGOUS

The appearance of color is affected by surrounding colors as well as by light sources. There are certain color combinations which have indisputable visual charisma, and finding them is not at all difficult when you examine the color wheel (*refer to page 30*) and the relationships on it.

The basic hues combine with special appeal when they are grouped with colors which are next door neighbors on the color wheel. A group of adjacent colors forms a color family or analogous color scheme. Examples of analogous groups are blues and greens, reds and violets, yellows and oranges. When colors next to each other on the wheel are used together, they are friendly and attractive to our eyes, but there is not a strong contrast.

(LEFT) *Blues, greens and blue-green form the heart of this eclectic color plan. Accents of primary red and yellow add excitement.* — AL EVANS

5-19

(ABOVE) *Fresh and contemporary, this color scheme suggests the magic of sun, sand and the tropics. Blues, blue-green, green and yellow dominate with accents of red adding to the light-hearted feeling.* — EDWARD NIETO

5-21

ANALOGOUS ◂ ◂ ◀ 87

(RIGHT) *Delicate varia-
tions of blue-green and
green against silver create
a dream-like setting for
dramatic dining.*
— JAMES ESSARY

5-18

5-20

(ABOVE) *Subtle changes of beautiful medium tone colors in the blue to blue-violet range with pure white on ceiling and in draperies make a memorable color statement.*
— NAN ROSENBLATT

(RIGHT) *The daring and dash of reds, oranges and deep yellows bathe these spaces with elegance and energy.*
— JANET SCHIRN

5-15

(ABOVE) *Blue, aqua and green cushions echo the waterfront view and the collection of glass.*
— AL EVANS

(INSET) *The colors of a glass collection dress a neutral room.*
— AL EVANS

COMPLEMENTARY

A second more dramatic system of combining colors is to pair colors which appear across from each other on the color wheel (*refer to page 30*). These are known as complementary color schemes. They create a tension through strong contrast as well as an attraction. If complements are too high in intensity, our eyes have trouble focusing and the images seem to tremble. In the 1960s, a group known as "Op" artists experimented with these unusual effects. Combined in less intense hues, complements form subtle color balances that are enormously pleasing to the eye. The most famous of these complementary relationships is red and green.

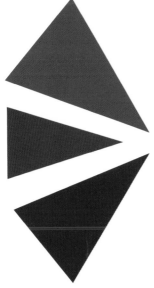

(RIGHT) *An exquisite tone of red-orange glows with warmth and is softened with accents of blue in this handsome room.*
— CHERYL DRIVER

5-14

5-6

(ABOVE) *Natural shades of leaf green and clay red tie the window view and the interior together in this fresh bath area. The towels and plants are part of the color plan.*
— LISE LAWSON

(LEFT) *Rust red and periwinkle blue counter each other for an unexpected and successful combination.*
— LISE LAWSON

(OPPOSITE) *Complementary blue-greens and rust-oranges effectively establish an unusual plan for this informal living space. The variety of tones from light to dark contributes to the success of the combination.*
— DAVID RIPP

5-7

5-13

(LEFT) *Gentle tones of red and green harmonize in this complementary color plan for a dining area. The area rug unifies the space.* — **PAT STOTLER**

(OPPOSITE) *Red and green are directly opposite each other on the color wheel, a balance that organizes the strong color combinations in this informal and stylish seating area.* — **ALLISON HOLLAND**

5-12

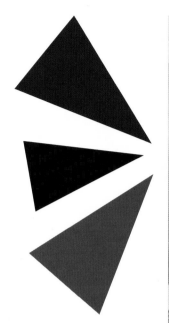

5-10

(ABOVE) *A deep blue-green wall treatment looks stunning with an oriental carpet. White woodwork and ceiling keep the room fresh.* — JAMES ESSARY

(LEFT) *A library with deep green walls and red leather upholstery. The red and white carpet and white ceiling softens the tension between red and green to create a satisfying balance.* — KENNETH HOCKIN

5-11

(RIGHT) *Golden tones of yellow in the wood paneling play to a soft violet background in the upholstery fabric. Accents of stronger yellow and peach punctuate the complementary theme.* — GLENNA COOK

(BELOW) *Deepest ink blue harmonizes with the red-orange of the oriental carpet and is cleanly framed with a white ceiling and woodwork.* — DAVID RIPP AND JUDY SKLAR SILBERSTEIN

5-9

5-1

(ABOVE) *A watermelon red and deep frost green palette is combined with dark wood finishes for a secure traditional bedroom.* — DEBRA BLAIR

5-3

5-4

(BOTH) *Matching intensities of red and green with a contrasting white ceiling and trim are never out of date but are definitely traditional. The balancing complementary colors are used in the connected living areas of this East coast home.* — ANTHONY ANTINE

NEUTRALS

Using neutrals does not mean not using color. Neutrals in interior design are colors too, and while not as blatantly emotional and attention-attracting as pure spectrum colors, they are capable of creating a wide range of effects from sleek sophistication to rustic casual. Any low intensity color that is used as a background for other accent colors, architectural features, furniture and objects in a space can be classified as a neutral.

Neutrals are practical; by changing accessories and fabrics the look of a space can be dramatically altered against the same neutral background. They are sensible in spaces which may change ownership frequently as well as in smaller areas where they can unify and create the illusion of greater space.

In homes around the United States, there are more color palettes dominated by the neutrals than any other single category. They are especially prevalent in the desert areas of the West and the Pacific Coast where the natural environment plays a major role in social trends and lifestyle.

The neutral palette begins with pure white and ends in jet black, with many interesting stops along the way. It includes greyed tones of all the primaries and secondaries and these range from a multitude of off-whites to deep, rich off-blacks. Professional interior designers frequently use colors such as cream, tan, taupe, camel, grey and sand. But they also develop blends which are as distinctive as their names: buttery cream, smoke grey, bone and khaki.

In the hands of a skilled amateur or a professional, neutral color schemes can be theatrical and dramatic. Either by contrasting black and white, or by using unique natural materials such as marble and highly figured wood veneers, a neutral interior need not be a boring interior. Neutral palettes are also used frequently as backgrounds for more intense colors and in spaces which feature art collections.

"I choose monochromatic neutral schemes for those who do not like clutter, the serious collector who does not want to distract from special objects and areas that require calm," observes New York interior designer Jean Valente.

And from Honolulu, designer Allison Holland says, "Always to balance out the brights. Great to use neutral in floors, ceiling, furniture wood tones and walls."

A practical consideration is offered by Chicago designer Robert Wiltgen, "I use neutral for backgrounds. Things are too expensive to change with the trends in home furnishings."

The following examples of homes from the East, West, South and Midwest demonstrate the versatility of these palettes and why they are so popular and timeless.

6-27

(ABOVE) *The distant foothills seem to roll into this California bedroom, welcomed by the monochromatic sand textiles and glowing rare wood veneers.* — ARTHUR PORRAS

(RIGHT) *White on white multiplies the impression of open space which the architecture demands in this unique Maryland home.* — RITA ST. CLAIR

(OPPOSITE) *Contemporary architectural lines of this residence in New York City are profiled with a palette of putty green, cocoa brown, smoke grey and tones of white.* — GAIL GREEN

6-26

(RIGHT) *White becomes a contemporary background for this serene bedroom.* — GAIL HAYES ADAMS

(BELOW RIGHT) *The soft white backgrounds frame an imposing view of Los Angeles, reflected in the blue bed cover.* — NORMAN WOGAN

(BELOW FAR RIGHT) *The soft and comforting low intensity color and light absorbing texture welcome guests and family.* — TERRELL GOEKE

(LEFT) *Reverence for unadorned natural materials is evident in many neutral interiors, especially in the Pacific region where it is a societal trend. The turquoise color of oxidized copper is a natural accent for backgrounds of sand and white.* — STEPHANIE WALTERS

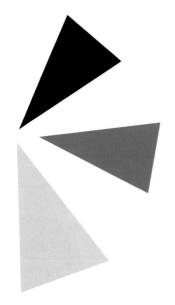

6-13

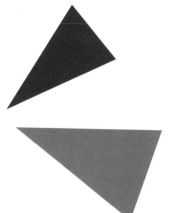

6-31

6-39

6-29

(ALL) *The color of natural materials and metal accents are the most appropriate palette for this apartment in a landmark Chicago building designed by one of the greatest masters of Modern, Mies van der Rohe. The intrinsic beauty of wood, marble, granite and natural fiber is celebrated by this disciplined use of white walls and ceilings.*

"I use neutral colors as a foundation for most of our schemes. I select neutrals and expand the range in values so that they move from the lightest shades to dark values."
— DONALD D. POWELL

(BELOW LEFT) *Putty and oatmeal with very restrained leaf green fabric provide deep visual comfort in keeping with this room's frequent use as a daily refuge.*
— SHELDON HARTE AND JOHN BROWNLEE

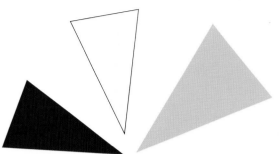

6-28   6-1

(BELOW RIGHT) *This putty grey monochromatic plan is understated and elegant. Textures and contrasting black neutrals add interest without disturbing a restful mood.* — MURIEL HEBERT

(BOTH) *Carefully planned details display a talent for varying neutrals from light to dark with hues such as taupe, raisin, nougat and either shiny or smokey black.*
— MICHAEL ANTHONY

6-23

(ABOVE) *This California bachelor's condominium was planned with an off-white background in various textures acting as a background for colorful accessories and plants.*
— DIANE JUST

(RIGHT) *All over almond-white presents a dramatic foil for the brightly colored artwork collected by this Florida family. The tinting of the white softens the mood of the room just enough to provide warmth without losing its contemporary zip. White, like many other colors, can be tinted to suit a wide range of moods.*
— VINCENT MOTZEL AND ARIEL SANS

6-36

(ABOVE & INSET) *Cosmopolitan reserve and discipline are reflected in this monochromatic grey plan. Within the monochromatic envelope, subtle surprises and visual relief can be carefully orchestrated.* — JOHN BERENSON

6-38

6-33

(LEFT) *The feature wall is painted and hand decorated in a swirling pattern, framed by the soft architecture of the stairway. Fabric color on the pillows brings the wall color into the main room and adds dimension to the plan.*
— KEVIN KOLANOWSKI

(BELOW LEFT) *Tan marble is a luxury, but the color is practical in a bathroom where watermarks plague darker colors. Black bathroom fixtures require very frequent cleaning and polishing.* — STEPHANIE WALTERS

(BELOW) *The stairway becomes a theatre with dramatic contrasting neutrals and a rich chocolate runway.*
— STEPHANIE WALTERS

(OPPOSITE) *Veils of white fabric, white walls and white trim are a dramatic stage for the stark black bed frame. The black fireplace marble and painted tables continue the rhythm of color.* — ANTHONY ANTINE

6-15

6-14

(ALL) *Neutrals fall back to let the quiet drama of marble and rare wood veneers enrich a Southern California home. This is painted with a palette of rich, natural materials.* — **ARTHUR PORRAS**

6-5

6-3

6-4

6-6

(RIGHT) *The architecture of the stairway is featured by profiling the shapes with backgrounds of texture and light. Black accents, wood tones, metal and dyed suede all provide neutral colors for this palette.*
— GAIL SHIELDS-MILLER

6-12

(RIGHT) *Soft cocoa, deep brown, wood tones and polished brass or gold with black design details are the palette for a warm and hospitable place to linger.*
— JEAN VALENTE

(BELOW) *Delicate white is interrupted only by the iron bed and warm neutral wood tones.* — JUDY R. MALE

(BELOW RIGHT) *Honey tones cheer the owners and guests in this cosmopolitan home, reflecting a healthy glow on most skin tones.* — GAIL GREEN

6-18

6-32

6-17

(LEFT) *The tension of geometric shapes in strong grey and black is a carefully phrased contemporary statement. Small points of other color add depth and tease the eye.*
— THOMAS ACHILLE

(BELOW) *'Furniture as Art' in extraordinary forms requires little embellishment. Neutrals with a light touch of color balances these unique objects.* — MARS AND RONN JAFFE

(OPPOSITE) *Sculptural and angular contemporary forms in an open black and white palette establish a classic tone for this dramatic stage-like space in Miami.*
— EDWARD NIETO

6-25

6-19

6-30

6-2

6-11

(ABOVE) *The California environment and lifestyle yields a predisposition toward soft neutral beige and the feature of naturally dramatic materials. Texture becomes important as a source for variety in this type of color plan.*
— BARBARA WOOLF

(LEFT) *Subtly mottled putty green walls match the upholstery fabric on the chaise and window seat. Black accents and white relief spark this comfortable sitting area.*
— VIVIAN IRVINE

6-22

(ABOVE) *The sunniest sunroom is predominantly white with cool green paint and decorated accents, a pastel floral print fabric and natural wicker.*
— MICHAEL ANTHONY

(RIGHT) *Earth tones in a casual living area are especially practical and inviting for a family's everyday use.* — ELAINE BASS

6-25

CREATING MOOD WITH COLOR

By Marsha Rae

7-4

Color has a profound effect on our mood. In clothing, interiors, landscape and even natural light, a color can change mood from sad to happy, from confusion to intelligence, from fear to confidence. It can actually be used to "level out" emotions or to create different moods.

Particular colors have very different effects on each individual. Response to a color may be influenced by a number of factors such as the body's need for a specific color, a sad or happy memory associated with a color, family history or current trends. The hope is that we will learn to "tune in" to our individual color responses and begin to create color palettes which will indeed nurture and inspire us.

In previous decades, certain colors or groups of colors dominated every palette. Now, in the 90s, the stopper is out and uniqueness and personal preference are really in!

There are no absolutes in the world of color. Some colors make you want to get out of your chair and "do." Others make you want to nestle down and read. Some colors are articulate and must be listened to. Others are very quiet. Some colors indicate that you have travelled or are well read. Yet others create a desire for closeness, intimacy and love.

Following are some of the most typical responses to various color groups.

(OPPOSITE) *Panoramic Western mountain views in this vacation retreat are a dramatic focal point balanced by the calming neutrals of fabric, wood, and paint.*
— MARSHA RAE

(RIGHT) *Warm black is a color that may be used to establish a feeling of nurturing protection.*
— DOTTY TRAVIS

7-3

NURTURING NEUTRALS

These colors create a sense of peace and well being. They foster quiet conversation with family and friends and can dispel loneliness. They can be used all by themselves or be combined with other "mood" colors. Throughout time, mankind has found a sense of peace and tranquility when in touch with "Mother Earth." It follows that the colors which impart a sense of warmth and serenity come directly from the earth. The other types of color palettes will often start from a foundation of nurturing neutrals.

In addition to the earth colors in the neutral group are colors associated with the sea, such as sand, shell, coral, pearl, stone and seaweed. Green is a color which helps us to adjust to new environments and situations. It will always be found among the "nurturing neutrals." Plant life colors with names like pine, lemon grass, fern, silver maple, bay laurel, moss green, mushroom, wheat and cornsilk also belong in this group. From the animal kingdom come colors described as fawn, leopard cub, field mouse, meadowlark and raccoon.

The blues represented here will range from winter sky to stream to midnight. And lastly, from grandma's kitchen come colors with descriptive names like buttermilk, maple sugar, coffee, ginger cookie, tea stain, peach cobbler and linen napkin.

Black is the color of protection so it may be used here. However, it is not one of the friendlier colors so it is best used in moderation. An exception is a palette which is largely warm blacks with other nurturing neutrals added as accents. This can express sophistication while remaining friendly and nurturing.

The neutrals are somewhat like the furniture while other palettes are more like accents or accessories. Some people enjoy more accessories than others, but everyone needs furniture. So it is with the neutrals in a palette.

(RIGHT) *A warm taupe is charming with red accents and white trim in this hospitable room complete with books and fireplace.*
— BARBARA AND MICHAEL ORENSTEIN

7-2

(LEFT) White is a color of purity and innocence, highly appropriate for this child's room. — **VIVIAN IRVINE**

(BELOW) Neutrals are relaxing, especially in the earth tones. An interesting collection of glazed and unglazed stoneware ceramics contributes to the natural mood. — **MARSHA RAE**

7-1

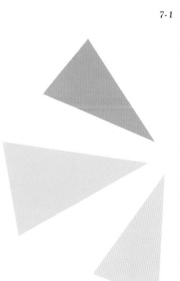

Intellectual — Sharp, Witty, Unique

These are colors which convey a message that the owner has travelled, is well-read and has something to say. These colors will command respect without being overbearing. Like the "nurturing neutrals," the "intellectual" palette will start with an earthy, warm base. Grey is a color which promotes creativity and will often be found in the foundation of an intellectual palette. These greys will be gentle and warm. They will function as a background for other colors in the palette and go unnoticed themselves. The level of contrast in the intellectual palette will appear less pronounced than in other palettes with lights and darks being bridged by intermediate tones.

Some tones of blue suggest communication and trust, so it will naturally be found in the intellectual palette. Related colors seem to be derived from elements in written communication such as India ink, parchment, vellum, charcoal, fountain pen blue and manilla. Navy blues will often find their way into these palettes, but the effect will be warm, and never cold and fragile.

Reds appear in the intellectual palette, but the shades will be earthy and complicated such as cranberry, burgundy and oxblood. A clear primary red would not appear in these palettes. Other colors which may be used in the intellectual palette are clove, cinnamon stick, celadon, driftwood, dolphin, snow white, sandalwood and puce (a deep red to grayish purple).

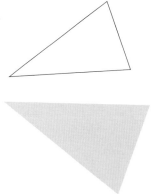

(ABOVE) *The mottled blue-green establishes a sophisticated, witty mood inspired by the classical antiquity of Pompeian frescoes at the Metropolitan Museum of Art in New York City. Wall covering is color-washed canvas, floor of pale limestone with green tumbled-marble inserts. Classical designs have been carved into the backsplashes and painted on the cabinets.* — NANCY MULLAN

7-7

7-8

(ABOVE) *A carefully mixed blue-green balances the mood of this sophisticated room.* — **DONNA VINING AND CYNTHIA STONE**

(LEFT) *This is an intellectual cranberry red in soft textures.* — **BILLY FRANCIS**

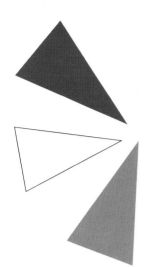

Playful — Exciting & Fun

Primary colors suggest a child's room begging for laughter and play. In an adult setting, these colors create a similar effect.

In order to create this look, a higher level of contrast is required. The contrast is achieved by balancing colors from around the wheel and by varying the intensities of the colors. Cool whites are often used in these palettes to separate the stronger hues and allow the eyes to articulate the space.

These playful, whimsical palettes create their own kind of music, like the sounds of children playing. There are highs and lows, lights and darks and always movement and activity. Used in active spaces within the home, a "playful" palette can add energy and vitality. If overdone, this type of palette becomes irritating and stressful.

The foundation for this type of palette is white. This could be anywhere from vanilla ice cream to snow drift, to winter moon. Then comes the energy of bubble gum pink, buttercup, chartreuse, teal, wintergreen and all the berry colors (blueberry, raspberry, strawberry, cherry, etc.), opalescents, pearlescents and the crayon colors. Many of these colors will be cool, and even in lighter tones there will be brightness and clarity.

The bottom line in creating this type of palette is that the colors should suggest a sense of freedom, play and downright fun!

7-10

(RIGHT) *Primary colors often are used to set a playful mood, but the black and white moo cows bring the message home.*
— Marsha Rae

(BELOW) *A joyful balance of primary colors invites activity and fun in this space for living.* — LISE LAWSON, CINDY GONNERING, NANCY FORBES, AND SUSAN STOCKTON

7-9

7-12

HEALING — REFRESHING & REJUVENATING

Like nurturing colors the "healing colors" also begin by getting in touch with nature. The first group of colors to be considered in this type of palette are the greens. Because they have the power to help us adjust to new environments, skillful designers use lots of plants and other forms of green in hotel lobbies, offices and restaurants. Healing greens may be warm or cool, but not muddy or mysterious like those in the intellectual palette. Any of the evergreen colors along with willow, artichoke and aloe work in these palettes.

Healing palettes also take inspiration from warm earth tones, especially colors from the autumn harvest, recalling berries, leaves and bittersweet. Fall flower colors also inspire this palette to include sunflower, marigold, cornflower, clover, nasturtiums and asters. Healing palettes usually contain contrast as well as a clarity of color that is inspiring. They will include a range of lights and darks but will never be muddy.

(LEFT) *The nurturing and rejuvenating colors of this pleasant eating area draw the natural colors inside.* — **LILA LEVINSON**

(RIGHT) *Floral colors and patterns create a rejuvenating environment.* — **BARBARA AND MICHAEL ORENSTEIN**

(BELOW) *Deep green is a comforting color in this California home.* — **CHERYL DRIVER**

7-13

7-11

ROMANTIC — SENSUAL

Ah, romance!! Many species including human beings attempt to attract the opposite sex with color. It is often an unconscious response to use color for this purpose. Red is the color of sex and lust and is often called the most romantic of colors. It is no accident that red is the chosen symbolic color for Valentine's Day.

In interior design, however, a less intense, softer tone of red is far more conducive to romance than the pure hue. Often referred to as pinks, these colors vary from cool to warm and from light to dark. Tones may be as delicate as dusty pink, shell or blush and as passionate as magenta, pomegranate and lipstick. Pinks have an interesting quality that seems to halt the body's ability to stay angry. Purple is another color which is definitively romantic because of its passionate, unpredictable and quixotic characteristics. Particularly in the medium to light tones such as wisteria, orchid and lilac, and even in deeper tones like Concord grape and wild plum; its poetic nature is apparent.

Paler, less intense tones of orange such as apricot and peach are often included in the romantic palette, suggesting purity and innocence. Blues in the romantic palette will be cool and inspired by water. Strong medium tones like periwinkle and light teal are popular choices.

The effects of color on mood will vary from individual to individual. An awareness of the emotions generated by different colors is helpful in planning personal palettes that will be pleasant to live with, but it must be understood that this information is not absolute. Each person's responses are inevitably fluid, and a color plan should not be unreasonably restricted by generalizations. Subtle changes in tone can increase or decrease the emotions evoked by a particular color, allowing it to be included in many diverse palettes.

7-14

7-15

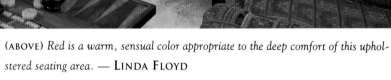

(ABOVE) *Red is a warm, sensual color appropriate to the deep comfort of this upholstered seating area.* — **LINDA FLOYD**

(OPPOSITE) *The romantic mood created with pink welcomes guests to this bedroom on the East coast.* — **BARBARA AND MICHAEL ORENSTEIN**

PERSONAL STYLE

There are no trends in color as important as personal style. Today, most designers draw from many historical periods as well as contemporary influences and mix them together to create unique personal spaces.

Many successful color schemes begin with a favorite shirt, an heirloom dish, a painting or a rug, something appreciated for its color. For example, a room can be built around the colors in a favorite oil painting. All fabrics and objects in the room can be done in a color which appears on the canvas. The result will be a complex, personal and successful space based on a simple plan. Another effective device for establishing a color scheme is repeating a feature fabric. In addition to draperies and upholstery coverings, fabric may be stretched on walls for a rich and satisfying tactile effect. The colors of a feature fabric may be repeated in walls, floor coverings and accessories. The view from the windows can also suggest color schemes for the interior spaces. Frank Lloyd Wright liked to plan interior colors which echoed perennial gardens on the surrounding grounds.

The most effective color palettes reflect and enhance the interests, collections and activities of the people who live there as well as architectural features. If the room is being designed for a person who appreciates and is interested in history, recreating the character of a past era may be important in establishing a color scheme. The art collector needs a neutral background to feature his or her prize possessions.

Color schemes have emotional messages too. On the following pages are examples of combinations which seem to convey the mood which the owners wish to create in their rooms: **lively** or **serene, bright** or **subtle, nostalgic** or **contemporary.**

RICH (ABOVE) *In a sophisticated New England home, this collection of black neoclassical furnishings is the focus, highlighted by the contrasting yellow walls.*
— JERILYN CLARKE-FORMAN

WHIMSICAL (OPPOSITE) *Vivid color from south-of-the-border repeated on painted furniture and ceramic tiles make a whimsical atmosphere in this kitchen.* — PAULA BERG

SENSITIVE (ABOVE) *Personal basket collection, polo mallets and natural pine cabinet reflect owner's appreciation of subtle natural textures.* — **ELAINE BASS**

BRIGHT (RIGHT) *A charming collection of porcelain boxes artfully displayed against a warm buttery neutral.* — **ALLISON HOLLAND**

STYLISH (OPPOSITE) *Color and texture of the desert and the ranch set a personal regional style.* — **PAULA BERG**

8-13

8-19

CONTEMPORARY (ALL) *A high-fashion contemporary home is created with white plus various tones of a rich red repeated throughout the interior.* — DAVID ESTREICH

8-21

8-20

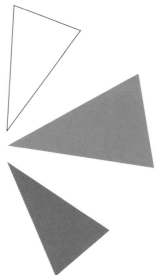

8-30

CULTURED (ABOVE) *Bold contemporary artwork and a grand piano are important personal signatures of these contemporary people. The all white backgrounds frame the most revealing clues to their personalities. People, art and music will dominate this space.* — FANNY HAIM AND BENNY FLINT

SUBTLE (RIGHT) *Primitive and contemporary works of art show up against greens and golds which are treated as neutrals in this setting.* — STEPHEN TOMAR AND STUART LAMPERT

8-6

8-27

DISCIPLINED (ABOVE) *The hard-edge geometric contemporary architecture is carried one step further with the discipline of a completely white color plan. A perfect foil for contemporary art.* — BARBARA ARKULES

INVIGORATING (RIGHT) *Ancient bottles, etched glass and mirror in a Chicago designer's own bath. The cool blue color feels clean, like fresh running spring water.* — JANET SCHIRN

8-29

8-7

REJUVENATING (ABOVE) *The garden view of this master-bath addition establishes a color theme carried out in tile, leafy patterned wallpaper, tapestry-covered chair, dark-green resin whirlpool tub and hardwood floor.*
— MARJORIE SLOVACK

SOPHISTICATED (Both) *The sparkling gold trim on the china and the gold washed flatware have inspired a gleaming color scheme with mirrors reflecting the soft warm neutrals of the upholstery and walls.*
— Carol Meltzer

8-10

8-11

8-12

SECURE (LEFT) *The warm wood tones of an exquisite antique tall case clock show beautifully against a neutral grey background wall and suggest rich traditional colors for other furniture and accessories.* — **DEBRA BLAIR**

ADVENTURESOME (BELOW) *An interest in primitive artifacts and textile designs is the key to understanding the foundation for this space. A multi-colored palette of primary and secondary colors, difficult to manage even by a professional, is anchored in neutral wall color and backgrounds. This variety of color and pattern reflects the designer's virtuosity and the owner's wide scope of interests in nature and culture.* — **DAVID RIPP AND JUDY SKLAR SILBERSTEIN**

8-32

8-26

DISCRIMINATING (ABOVE) *A dining room gallery for the connoisseur in a traditional shade of red.* — STEPHEN TOMAR AND STUART LAMPERT

SERENE (LEFT) *This owner enjoys being immersed in tradition with a red toile and complementary colored linen suggesting a European ancestry.* — DAN CARITHERS

8-18

PERCEPTIVE (RIGHT)

*A favorite painting can be
the arbiter of all other colors in the room, allowing
an eclectic assortment of
furniture and accessories.*
— RODGERS-MENZIES

8-4

8-2

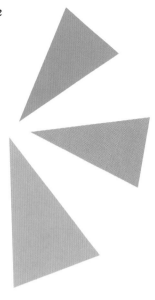

REFRESHING (ABOVE) *Outdoor colors flow into interior spaces. Colors of ceramics collection relates to natural beauty.* — **LISA ROSE**

STIMULATING (RIGHT) *The owner's obvious interest in primitive art and painted furniture has determined the color palette of this cheerful room.*
— **ALLISON HOLLAND**

8-8

YOUTHFUL (ABOVE) *Neutral buff and blue are the perfect light and bright background for a child's toy collection.* — **MARILYNN LUNDY**

NOSTALGIC (LEFT) *Architectural features can sometimes suggest color arrangements; in this case, strong colors in built-ins set off owner's cherished collections.* — **ALLISON HOLLAND**

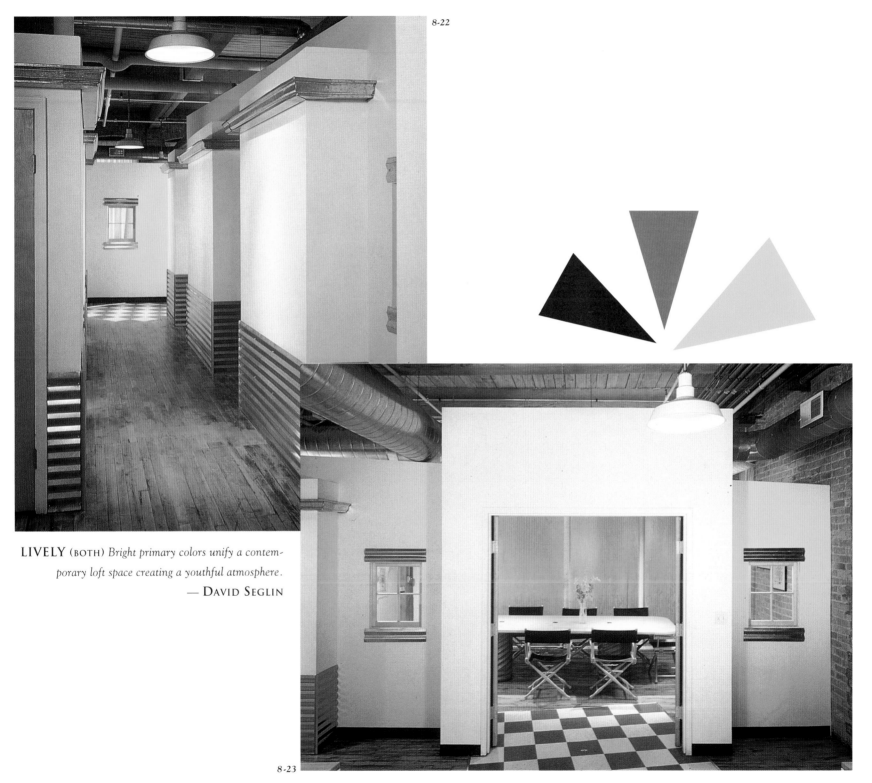

LIVELY (BOTH) *Bright primary colors unify a contemporary loft space creating a youthful atmosphere.*
— DAVID SEGLIN

8-22

8-23

COMFORTING (ABOVE) *Assorted pillows in a variety of textures and colors suggest a light and bright comfortable multi-colored palette. Details make the difference!* — **ALLISON HOLLAND**

CHEERFUL (RIGHT) *A precious collection of Majolica ware on a table creates textural interest and is enhanced by pale yellow walls.* — **ALLISON HOLLAND**

DISTINCTIVE (OPPOSITE) *The owner's table service creates a color palette for the room with carpet, walls and accessories reflecting the basic theme.* — **ANTHONY ANTINE**

INTELLECTUAL (RIGHT) *A lifetime of family, friends and books that have really been read are clues to authentic quality. Beware of anyone who buys books to decorate a shelf! The colors are rich and warm like many of the well worn book bindings.* — JANET SCHIRN

INVITING (BELOW) *Deep tones of wood paneling provide a warm and inviting dominant color and harmonize with the other deep colors of furniture and accessories.* — DEBRA BLAIR

8-14

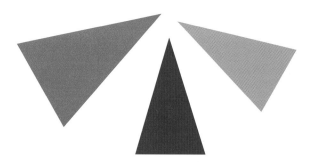

8-1

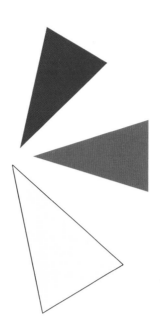

WORLDLY (ABOVE) *A neutral background features an exquisite Oriental screen. Accents in complementary red and green accessories echo most vivid and predominant screen colors.* — ILLYA HENDRIX AND THOMAS ALLARDYCE

WISTFUL (RIGHT) *For those who appreciate styles of the past and wish to immerse themselves in the aura of another time, these mellow colors look like faded antique textiles and glow with memories.* — BECKI COOK

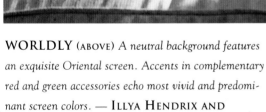

8-33

ALTERING COLOR

This chapter presents options for altering color to help in creating your personal style. The following are color swatches of the three primary hues and the three secondary hues demonstrating different ways of altering each basic color.

The first row on each page will show gradations of the basic color formed by adding white. The second row on each page will show gradations of the basic color formed by adding black. The third row on each page will show gradations of the basic color formed by adding the complementary color opposite it on the color wheel.

RED:
Gradually adding white

RED:
Gradually adding black

RED:
Gradually adding its complementary color

BLUE:
Gradually adding white

BLUE:
Gradually adding black

BLUE:
*Gradually adding its
complementary color*

YELLOW:
Gradually adding white

YELLOW:
Gradually adding black

YELLOW:
*Gradually adding its
complementary color*

GREEN:
Gradually adding white

GREEN:
Gradually adding black

GREEN:
*Gradually adding its
complementary color*

VIOLET:
Gradually adding white

VIOLET:
Gradually adding black

VIOLET:
Gradually adding its complementary color

ORANGE:
Gradually adding white

ORANGE:
Gradually adding black

ORANGE:
Gradually adding its complementary color

ACKNOWLEDGEMENTS

Interior Designer's Showcase of Color has become a reality because of a concept, a plan, and the cooperation of many outstanding professionals. We feel very fortunate to have had support and encouragement from all over the United States, through our association with Vitae Publishing. And we know that the book is more comprehensive because of this enthusiasm for our idea.

In addition to those designers who contributed photography of their work for the project we would like to acknowledge the following designers who responded to our survey, sharing their personal expertise on the use of color in interior design:

Michael Anthony	Orlando Diaz-Azcuy	Kathleen Dickelman	Donald Powell and
MB Affrime	T. Keller Donovan	Lise Lawson	Robert Kleinschmidt
Anthony Antine	Lois Esformes	Ellen Terry Lemer	Marsha Rae
Barbara Arkules	Danielle Garr	Sally Sirkin Lewis	Janet Schirn
Douglas Bartoli	David Gentry	Marilyn Lundy	Ronald Schwarz
Elaine Bass	Gail Green	Carol Meltzer	David Seglin
Connie Beale	Victoria Hagan	Gail Shields Miller	Rita St. Clair
Debra Blair	Wes Hageman	Doris Oster	Jean Valente
Timothy Button	Richard V. Hare	Stephanie Parisi	Lisa Weitz
Sharon Campbell	Dennis Haworth	Walters	Margot Wilson
Peter Charles	William Hodgins	Charles Pavarini III	John Robert Wiltgen
Steve Chase	Allison Holland	and Elizabeth Cole	Barbara Woolf
Jerilyn Clarke	Noel Jeffrey	Arthur Porras	B. Jordan Young
Jane Crary	Diane Just	Janie Petkus	
Larry Deutsch	Kerry Joyce	Warren Platner	

We especially thank designers Suzanne Tucker and Timothy Marks for providing the cover photograph taken by John Vaughan. We also acknowledge Cynthia Vandecar, Amy Aves, Claudia Rouse, Alison Aves, Christine Humes, and Dee Dudick for their support and assistance with the research, correspondence, proofing and indexing details of the project.

Our friends at Rockport Publishers, Inc. have been a pleasure to work with. Barbara States and Rosalie Grattaroti have conscientiously shepherded us through the details of the process, and designer Laura Herrmann is friendly, talented, patient and thoroughly professional. It is especially gratifying to end a project with new knowledge, new skills, new appreciations, and new friends.

INDEX OF DESIGNERS

INDEX OF PHOTOGRAPHERS

Stites, William
Rowayton, CT
2-17 — p. 39   *2-55* — p. 59   *5-11* — p. 96

Swain, John
Sacremento, CA
7-4 — p. 120   *7-1* — p. 123

Szanik, George
Los Angeles, CA
6-11 — p. 118

Taggart, Fritz
Los Angeles, CA
1-4 — p. 9

Terzes, Andrew C.
Grand Rapids, MI
3-25 — p. 73   *3-26* — p. 73

Thompson, Philip
Los Angeles, CA
8-26 — p. 143

Vail, Baker
New York, NY
1-18 — p. 18   *4-15* — p. 84

Vander Schuit, Joan
San Diego, CA
6-15 — p. 110

Vaughan, John
San Francisco, CA
2-8 — p. 33   *3-16* — p. 71   *5-20* — p. 89
2-21a — p. 40   *4-3* — p. 77   *6-2* — p. 118
2-26 — p. 43   *5-14* — p. 91   *6-19* — p. 116

Vertikoff, Alex
Los Angeles, CA
1-10 — p. 14

Vitale, Peter
New York, NY
1-8 — p. 11   *1-13* — p. 13
1-12 — p. 13   *1-14* — p. 6

Wakely, David
San Francisco, CA
2-47 — p. 55

Wesnofske, Christopher
New York, NY
2-3 — p. 31   *4-5* — p. 76   *8-9* — p. 146

White, Charles S.
Los Angeles, CA
8-6 — p. 138

Wilkins, Frieda
Wilmington, NC
1-33 — p. 27

Williams, Sandra
San Diego, CA
6-23 — p. 108

Yochum, James
James Yochum Photography
Chicago, IL
1-17 — p. 15   *6-29* — p. 103
5-15 — p. 89   *8-28* — p. 150

All transparencies and/or photographs reproduced in the book have been accepted on the condition that they are reproduced with the knowledge and prior consent of the photographer concerned, and no responsibility is accepted by the publisher or printer for any infringement of copyright or otherwise arising out of publication thereof.

BIBLIOGRAPHY

Anderson, Donald M., *Elements of Design*. New York: Holt, Rinehart and Winston, 1961.

Best From the Interior Design Hall of Fame. Grand Rapids, Michigan: Vitae Publishing, Inc., 1992.

Birren, Faber, *Color and Human Response*. New York: Van Nostrand Reinhold, 1978.

Birren, Faber, *Color for Interiors*, Historical and Modern. New York: Whitney Library of Design, 1963.

Chijiiwa, Hideaki, *Color Harmony*. Rockport, Massachusetts: Rockport Publishers, Inc. 1989.

Color Sourcebook. Rockport, Massachusetts: Rockport Publishers, Inc., 1989.

Color Sourcebook II. Rockport, Massachusetts: Rockport Publishes, Inc., 1989.

Crane, Catherine C., *What Do You Say To A Naked Room?* New York: The Dial Press, 1979.

Dondis, Donis A., *A Primer of Visual Literacy*. Cambridge, Massachusetts: The MIT Press, 1973.

Gail, Ian and Irvine, Susan, *Laura Ashley Style*. New York: Harmony Books, 1987.

Krippner, Stanley and Daniel Rubin, editors, *The Kirlian Aura*. New York: Anchor Books, 1974.

Luscher, Max, *The Luscher Color Test*, translated and edited by Ian Scott. New York: Washington Square Press, 1969.

Mc Kim, Robert H., *Thinking Visually*. Palo Alto, California: Dale Seymour Publications, 1980.

Preble, Duane and Sarah, *Artforms*. Fourth Edition. New York: Harper and Row, 1989.

Sargent, Walter, *The Enjoyment and Use of Color*. New York: Dover Publications, Inc., 1964.

Showcase of Interior Design; Eastern Edition, Midwest Edition, Pacific Edition, Southern Edition. Grand Rapids, Michigan: Vitae Publishing, 1989-1993.

After sharing undergraduate courses in art and English at Albion College in Michigan, John and Melanie Aves have been involved in art and design throughout their careers and their thirty-year marriage. John's work has centered on the field of communications including advertising, public relations and publishing. Melanie is a painter and an art educator; having earned a Masters degree from Calvin College. She is currently teaching courses at East Grand Rapids High School and Grand Valley State University. The Aves have three daughters that live in Grand Rapids, Michigan.